FIFTY POEMS

Fifty Poems

Liana Quill

The Mississippi Review Poetry Series
Hattiesburg 2010

Published by the *Mississippi Review*, Hattiesburg, MS 39406

Manufactured in the United States of America

10 9 8 7 6 5 4 3 2 1

ISBN 978-0-9842652-1-3

ISSN 0047-7559

Mississippi Review Volume 37 Number 3 ~ Book 2 of 3

Mississippi Review is published twice a year by the Center for Writers, The University of Southern Mississippi (AA/EOE/ADAI), 118 College Drive, #5144, Hattiesburg, MS 39406-0001. Editor: Frederick Barthelme. Managing Editor: Rie Fortenberry. Associate Editors: Angela Ball, Steven Barthelme, Julia Johnson. Assistant Editors: Lynn Watson, Elizabeth Wagner, Beth Couture. Subscription rates: $15 per year for individuals, $32 for institutions. Foreign subscriptions $10 per year additional. Single copies $9. *Mississippi Review* wishes to acknowledge the kind support of the National Endowment for the Arts. The views expressed herein are those of the authors, not the editors or sponsors. Printed in the United States of America by McNaughton & Gunn, Inc., P.O. Box 10, Ann Arbor, MI 48176. Distributed in the United States by Ubiquity Distributors, 607 Degraw St., Brooklyn, NY 11217. Archive available through JSTOR. Indexed by *Humanities International Complete*. Special thanks to Dara Wier for selecting the 2010 *Mississippi Review* Poetry Series winners.

Contents

FADING FATHERS   9

BROTHER'S KEEPER   10

CHERITH   11

ALL MIST FROM THENCE   12

CHANGE FOR   13

DEEP NESTED   14

LANDING LIGHT FADES   15

INUNDATE   16

SHE ENDS, WITH: 17

1615 CORTLAND ROAD   18

PRETTY TAIL LIKE   19

ASH-HEADED   20

FLINTHEAD   HISS   21

WASH THEIR HANDS OVER   22

SAND STRUCK   23

MOTH FLIES FROM   24

IRIS WHITE   25

MOTHERED PEARL   26

FORGED   27

SING WATER   28

HER FATHER BUILT   29

COURLAN   30

CONIFER WEDGED   31

BY WHITE STRIPE   32

UNDERNEATH RAIN COMES   33

SILVER THAT WERE TAKEN   34

THE WINDOW'S GLASS   35

EASTERN   36

UNSPOKEN   37

SEA-   38

BARNACLE HATCHED   39

BIND   40

WHICKERING   41

SOIL SOWN   42

LEFT HIS   43

LEATHERBACK —   44

LATE AUTUMN RAIN   45

SISTERTWIN   46

THREE   47

LOOK AFTER,   48

FLIGHT FEATHERS,   49

FOR BROTHER HEART: 50

METALLIC   51

THE YOUNGEST   52

MARCH 19, MAY 1   53

NEVADA   54

STRETCH 'CROSS COUNTRY   55

CORNER OF BUSH AND GOUGH   56

BLADE   57

SWEET SUNG   58

NOTES   60

ABOUT THE AUTHOR   61

TO R, FROM L

fading fathers

          fruit tree seed.
over-Ocean
          limed Linnet.

brother's keeper

   circle
          lesser-linen
                nested.
repentance:
          cleft

Cherith

knowledge   raven's
       stone
          in flame

All Mist From Thence

Of sea-crow
fallen,
fruit offered:

our mortal way.

change for

        Rahab-light
            bent,
  and candle
  lit

deep nested and

                resurrected to
        celandine
                    sight.
    mud made

Landing light fades

a trunk,
            seven magpies,
blue with
age.

inundate

   rain crow
       yellow lidded.
Broken,

his nestless nose

She ends, with:

    wire-tap feet
            cut blue.

woodscolt, and
          hooked chance

1615 Cortland Road

pigeoned eaves,
call a name.

absolution parted

pretty tail like

                hazel twigs.
     bone
          cheek:
     window tapped.

ash-headed

faithful
wanderings,

    spider egg or
    bayberries

flinthead   hiss

—young, eaten—
            from flame
fly.

wash their hands over

lowing muted
                    —familial
flock,
                blackened.

sand struck

    verdin moon
        —clouded
           over
  daughter-eyes

moth flies from

     frog-mouthed
night jarring
    cries wake
        infidelity

iris white

   gap packed — twig and soil
snails
  shared

mothered pearl

her   daffodils
        bent,
enclosed by gold-ringed eye

forged

    bobwhite
hatched
      firm ground-lings;

        submerging.

sing water

dipper stitch
                              fade down:
mossbacked jade

her father built

    mohave daffodil;
        ladderbacks eye bovine—
lapping.

courlan

       wails
       wade deeper
fading to
 marsh brown

conifer wedged

    with hickory nut

    hawkweed,
        walk down

by white stripe

rowan hid,
                    heart fed
        his words:
spoken.

underneath rain comes:

    bird teeth,
            lavender pressed pane.
tin hammered oak,
    lantern lit.

silver that were taken

sky set.
          piannet,
  unwept.

The window's glass

Doubt in
        Mountain mending.

duplicity,
     Moon   lit.

Eastern

clawed hands   grip
            owl.

Moistened green silk,
        starling mended

unspoken

        dog rubbed
          golden
            stars, for
Sofia's secret,
     tarnish.

sea-

          stare left
                    lavendered
          Alaw's single stone

barnacle hatched

fig fed
liver
            inflamed

bind

    epaulettes red
         with
sedge.
blackfeet, un-seared

whickering

against cloud-Dusk,
              crooked limbs clasp
   brown-blotched down

soil sown

pheasant eye
        burns
                green:
mirrored end

left his

Stonechat scotch(ed)

  the nestwool,
  unbound.

leatherback—

    egged eyes
bulge uphill.

late autumn rain

Grounded
          swift—
     chimney bred.
Now, hermit caved.

Sistertwin

Grayed
          Plover steps
through boreal snow

Three

            lovebirds fester.
teeth   stuck
    with   bone dust.

look after,

        iris brown,
slate winged
        winter twin— frost edged.

flight   feathers,

                              lost
restitution
                crèche-thread

for brother heart:

      shearwaters   share
an emptied nest

metallic

       chirp
   through glass:
             answered,
by crocus fed

The Youngest

        ashed, and oily.
smell of
him
    sticking to our
                        wrists

March 19, May 1

    Depression nested
rusted   grouse,
    yolk fed.

Nevada

camel-glow   over
        towhee-ed pieces:
     bones   in a box.

stretch 'cross country

 born under
quick cloudsore—
cut   bent   or
        worn.

Corner of Bush and Gough

        sunrise song
              —once a warning
      fielded exaltation

  steps   away

blade

will pierce
     mary blue and
wood-bellied
        nest:
      razed

sweet sung

    thicket edged with
        Bloodstuck cheek
thistle down,
    half emptied

NOTES

All Mist From Thence
Paradise Lost, IV, 194-196

change for
Joshua 6:25

unspoken
Statue of St. John of Nepomuk, Charles Bridge, Prague

sea-
Branwen of Wales

Three
Ivan Albright's painting

Corner of Bush and Gough
Trinity Episcopal Church, San Francisco

About the Author

A native Virginian, Liana Quill is currently writing and teaching in Prague.